Father Ike's Stories for Children

Father Ike's Stories For Children

Teaching Christian Values
Through Animal Stories

REV. ISAIAS POWERS, CP

TWENTY-THIRD PUBLICATIONS
Mystic, Connecticut

Twenty-Third Publications
P.O. Box 180
Mystic CT 06355
(203) 536-2611

ISBN 0-89622-370-1
Library of Congress Catalog Card Number 88-50332

Edited by Andrea Carey
Cover design by William Baker
Illustrations by Bette Schlosser

CONTENTS

INTRODUCTION

I must insist that this book is written for children, ages 9–12. If grownups want to read these pages, okay...but they must be quiet and behave themselves. I'm talking to young people—first of all, to me, when I was that age, and then to others who are that age now.

I've been a priest for over 25 years. Most of that time, I've given parish missions and retreats. On the missions, I have one talk for Grades 1–3, another for Grades 4–6, and another for Grades 7–8.

This book of animal stories is the one I give for Grades 4–6. I tell the stories and ask the boys and girls to give me ideas about what the stories mean—in terms of their growing up. The responses have been great. Much of what I have put down under the heading "Moral of the Story" have been their ideas.

I want to thank them, wherever they are now.

Almost all the stories have been part of my own experience. They really happened to me. I have remembered them as honestly as I can. The mind, however, can play funny tricks when it tries to go back into things that took place many years ago. To the best of my knowledge, these stories are true. I want to give special thanks to my illustrator. Without her, the action would have died down. With her help, it zings along.

I hope you enjoy reading these pages as much as I enjoyed writing them. When you finish the book, please pray for me so that I can, little by little, grow up, too.

The Dog
Who Demanded Too Much

The Story: Some years ago, I was invited to give a retreat for college students in the Catskill Mountains. I got there a day ahead of time and took a good long walk. On my way back, in a corner of the property, I came upon a large St. Bernard dog. He was penned in. He wasn't exactly cramped for space. He had a lot of room to move around. But he was stuck in that quarter acre of his own world.

Obviously, he didn't get too many visitors. When I got close, his tail started to wag furiously and he squealed for joy at seeing me. As soon as he stood up on his hind legs, paws on the fence, he was taller than I was.

Oh, was he glad to find a friend! I petted him and we talked for some time. (That is, I did the talking; he kind of gurgled back.) I love dogs. And he was a very likeable one. I didn't have to wash for a week! His large tongue was licking my face so hard, I thought I was being doused by a mop.

After a while, time was up. I began to leave. Then the dog started whimpering and whimpering...asking me to come back. I felt sorry for him, so I did go back. But not for long. I got tired of it; and then I realized I had to go. I left him, this time, for good.

As I went back to the house, I had the feeling that if I gave him 24 hours a day of my attention, he would have wanted 25!

A strange thing happened after that. Remember, I do

like dogs. And I liked this one in particular. I really did. But I never went back to see him, even though I was there for three more days. He wanted too much of me. He was too greedy for my attention. There was no way that I could really please him. He drained my energy because his needs were too great, and I couldn't bear to listen to that whimper of his if I went back and then left him again.

That's the end of my story. What's the lesson that it teaches in human terms? What does that St. Bernard

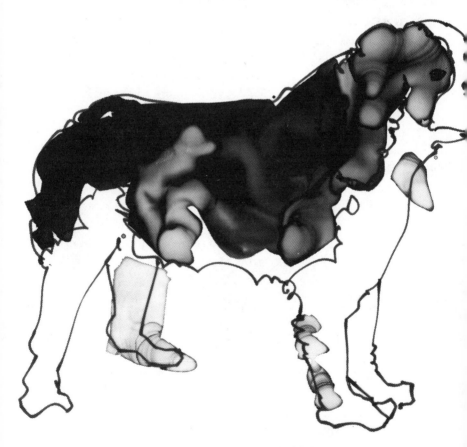

dog tell you about growing up, about what *not* to be?

This is an easy one to figure out. I'll just relax a couple of minutes while you think about it. Then I'll come back and put it in other words.

MORAL OF THE STORY

Yes, you're right. The moral of the story is "Don't become too demanding of your friends. Don't turn into a person like that St. Bernard dog of the Catskill Mountains."

I'm sure you've heard your parents complain about some person who acts like this. Maybe the person was called "that pest who keeps calling me on the telephone" or something like that. Certain people are real "drags."

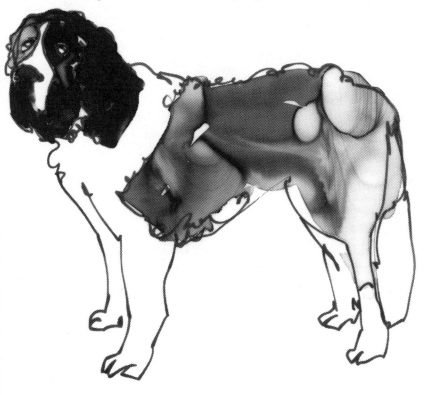

They drain your energy because they demand too much of your time, and too much of *you*.

Also, there are certain individuals who are very jealous. Maybe you've heard teenagers, or older people, talk about them. Maybe it's a girl who gets mad because her boy friend spends too much time with his buddies and not enough time with her. Maybe it's a boy who makes a scene any time his girl friend even talks to another boy. Maybe it's parents who are so possessive of their children—so "clinging"—they won't let their children have any time for themselves. Things like that.

Life can get terribly uncomfortable when you always have to worry about those people who try to hang on to you (like the St. Bernard dog who tried to hang on to me)...and then they whimper, or whine, or try to make you feel guilty somehow when you spend time with anything else but them!

Don't ever turn into a person like that St. Bernard dog. Be easy on your friends. Do your best *not* to become jealous of other people. And don't get bitter about the time they take doing things that you don't care about. Don't lay "guilt trips" on anybody. And don't go around thinking that you "own" anybody.

It's okay for babies and little children to make demands on their parents and older brothers and sisters. It's okay for them to whimper and whine if they don't get their way. I guess it's okay for St. Bernard dogs to do it, too. But it's not okay for you. If you make sure you don't put too many demands on people, you will grow up the way you want to, and you'll always have a lot of good friends.

The Eyeball of a Fish
("Eat it, or we're dead!")

The Story: It may seem like stretching things a bit to call this an animal story—fish are fish, animals are animals — but I guess fish are in the animal kingdom somehow. Also, this story isn't even about a live fish. It's a "fish dinner fish"—baked in the oven and served up on a platter, head and tail and all. And actually, it's not even about the whole fish that was lying there. It's only about a part of him—one of his eyeballs.

But it's a good story and I want to tell it. Long ago, in 1946, I was a soldier in Nanking, China. Years have a way of causing slippage to the memory. But there was one night in Nanking when I went to a fancy banquet that I'll never forget.

Three of us were invited to a big dinner in the center of that city. My two friends were both Chinese-American soldiers who knew the language and knew the customs. They saved my life. I don't know the reason why we went to the dinner. All the other guests were Chinese officers and their wives. It was a large gathering. The host was the mayor of the city. (He was also a general in the army.)

The Chinese eat differently from the way we do. Servants (who were soldiers) put a bowl of rice in front of each guest. There were about 20 different plates of delicious foods placed in the middle of a big table. We all helped ourselves to what we wanted. It was great.

However, I sat next to the general. He paid a lot of attention to me. He liked me, for some reason. (I never did find out why.) But the fact was that he liked me. He wanted to *show* me that he liked me; and he wanted me to relax and like him, too. So he reached out with his chopsticks and speared the eyeball of that baked bass, lying on a plate in dead-center of the table. I don't know whether it was a small-mouthed bass or a large-mouthed bass. But I certainly would call it a big-*eyed* bass. The eye was the size of a pebble, and it seemed to be glaring at me from the end of the chopsticks.

The general was smiling at me, urging me to eat it. I didn't say a word. I was too scared. My blood (they told me later) rushed away from my face. My stomach was turning over. I leaned over to my friend (who knew the customs) and I whispered, "What'll I do?" I definitely did *not* want to eat that eyeball, but I didn't know how to say no in a kind way.

My friend whispered back (he was scared, too) and said, "Eat it, or we're dead!"

You see, the gift of a fish's eyeball was a sign of

friendship, an honor, an offer of great respect. It would have been an insult for me to pass it up. It would have been so insulting—as my friends told me later—that the soldiers might have been angry enough to shoot us.

Don't ask me if I ate it. I'm still alive, I must have! I remember swallowing the slimy thing as I would a large pill. And then I smiled at my new friend. It didn't hurt me. As I said, I'm still alive.

Now what's the moral to this story? What does it say to you about growing up? Take all the time you need to think about it. I know you'll come up with one or two ideas. I'll be back and add another one.

MORAL OF THE STORY
I'm sure you've already figured out the first lesson. Sometimes, for the sake of peace and harmony, you have to do things you really don't want to do. Things like homework for school, jobs around the house, other boring stuff. It could be that you have to eat some food you don't like. Maybe it's not as bad as the eyeball of a bass. Maybe it's broccoli. You don't like to do these things. Nobody said you always have to like it. But you do it. That's life.

There's another point, another moral. Different people have different ways of showing love and friendship. Different countries have different customs. Even in the same country—even in the same family—nobody is exactly alike. We even have different kinds of hugs. People of different ages—athletes in different sports— have a variety of ways of shaking hands.

Part of growing up is the ability to respect the differences of others. Sometimes, you will get uncomfortable when certain individuals show that they like you, and want you to like them. You may think they "aren't doing it right" because that's not the way *you* would do it.

Back off a little bit. And back down. Don't pay too much attention to yourself in these cases. Don't demand that everybody, always, "do things the way you want them to." Try to look at it from the other person's point of view.

As long as people aren't trying to "use" you or trying to talk you into doing bad things, you should accept their way of telling you they want to be your friend. Let them do so. You may even get to enjoy their customs.

Respecting other people's differences is part of growing up.

Don't Honk at a Moose

The Story: This is a story about moose. All of them. The ones I speak about are in Canada.

You know what a moose looks like. They are an "army tank" on stilts. And their antlers weigh almost as much as the rest of them. It gives me a headache just thinking about wearing a hat like that. But they seem to have adjusted.

As a rule, moose have nothing to do with humans. They don't like us. They don't want to be hunted down, of course. So they are afraid of humans with guns. But even without guns, they'd just as soon steer clear of us. "Live and let live" is their motto.

There is one situation, however, when they definitely dislike humans. It's when they are licking up salt from the country roads. They don't want to be interfered with, and they don't like the sound of a honking horn!

I never actually saw a moose bust up a car for honking. But when I was a priest in Sudbury, Ontario, I heard about it. Imagine the scene: The season is early spring. The location is any narrow road, up north. All winter long, salt has been spread on the roads. The winters are cold up there. The ice is bad. So a lot of salt is laid down to keep the roads from becoming slippery. Then comes springtime and the sun melts the ice and snow, but the salt stays there, all its work finished.

Well, moose need salt just like everybody else. And

it's been a hard winter. So out they come from the woods and swamps, and they start licking the salt from the road, contented as you please.

Sometimes they take a "broadside" position while they are concentrating on their food. When this happens, there's no way for a car to get around them. If you happen to be in a car, you're stuck.

Natives who know the ways of a moose keep their cool. They turn off the motor and simply wait until lunch is over, and the moose walks off.

But strangers do a dumb thing. They think a moose is like an overgrown dog on the highway, or a duck, or a kitten, or a child playing in the street. They get impatient with the delay. They start yelling out the window. Then, worst of all, they start honking their horn. The moose turns around and glares. The driver honks again and yells, "Get outta the road!"

Now the moose can't stand the sound of a honking horn. *Any* horn. He charges at the sound. The action is like a big bulldozer going about 25 miles an hour armed with 300 pounds of antlers, and the animal rams into the hood of the car, causing the whole front to squeeze up like an accordion.

Then the moose trots off. He didn't even get

hurt. But the car is totaled. Nothing for the driver to do but wait for the tow truck—a wait that is much longer than if he just took it easy while the moose finished his salt-lick.

Now what's the moral to the story? Don't tell me "Don't honk at a moose." I already told you that. What's the moral in terms of you, growing up the right way? Take your time. You know it has to do with patience and "stretching your understanding." Think about it.

MORAL OF THE STORY
I know you thought up something interesting. I can't hear what you're saying, but I know it was good. Stay with it. Now I want to add my idea to yours. I want to link this story with the last one—the one about the eyeball of the fish.

Just as different people have different ways of showing their love and friendship, so do people have different ways of showing anger and frustration. The Mayor of Nanking, China, showed his love for me by giving me that eyeball to eat. It wasn't my way of saying "I like you"; but I had to accept him for who he was and what he was trying to do.

Likewise, you wouldn't get mad if the driver of a car honked at you to get out of the road. Maybe you'd get a little annoyed, but you wouldn't get as mad as a moose gets.

It's the same thing with your family and friends. Sometimes your mother and dad get upset by what you do. As far as you're concerned, you wouldn't get so upset if they did the same to you. So you're puzzled by it and wonder why they get so hot under the collar. But different things get different people irritated.

And that goes the other way around, too. There are

some things that cause you to get angry at your parents because of what they are doing. For instance, maybe you yell at your mother for the way she packed your lunch. Maybe you get sore at your dad because he wants things done so perfectly. Maybe you make a big scene because your brother or sister takes too much time in the bathroom. Sometimes they can't understand *you*...why you get so upset over things that don't bother them nearly as much as they bother you.

Same thing with your friends. You get mad at them because of something they do. They don't understand why you get so worked up about it. On the other hand, they get impatient with you for some habit you have and you don't know why they make such a big thing out of it.

Part of growing up is learning to understand that we are all different. People have different ways of showing their love and friendship. And they have a set of different things that cause them to get mad. Nobody is built the same way.

So learn to be patient with people who sometimes blow off steam for reasons that seem to you to be as dumb as a Canada moose charging into a car because he can't stand the sound of a horn.

That's the way of a moose. That's the way of life. It's all part of growing up.

Farm Cats Need Milk

The Story: This story goes back almost 40 years. Some facts I don't remember. But there are some things I am still sure of. I'm sure of the fat sides of one particular holstein cow. I'm sure there were two cats on the farm. I still remember how the barn looked in the late afternoon, when the sun creeped inside the open door, near the place where I was milking cows.

I think I was a freshman in high school. It was in the early 1940s. I volunteered to help as a farmhand. I was a city boy doing my best on a small dairy farm near Oswego, NY.

One job I liked the best. My boss, the farmer, told me to give the cats a squirt of milk every time they asked for it. This was fun. The two cats seemed to know exactly when I would be milking this one cow.

There I'd be, sitting on a little stool. And I'd start milking into the pail pressed to my knees. Then those two cats would show up. After they watched me for awhile, they'd start yelling for lunch. It wasn't an ordinary *meeow*. It was a different kind of cry, more of an *eeeeeooh*. I couldn't miss what they wanted. They were calling for the "hose" of the cow's udder to be aimed at them. Sometimes I teased them, with words I thought were funny—like "No free lunch today!" or "The price of milk is 10 cents a squirt!"

They knew the routine. With supreme confidence that they were going to get what they wanted, they would call out once more. Then I'd aim the milk in their direction. It would go on a high arc and end up in their mouths. The biggest one took the first drink. Then the other. They never missed a drop. Then they'd spend a minute or two licking off their whiskers. Sometimes one squirt was enough. Sometimes the procedure was repeated. It depended on their mood and their appetite and how many rats they killed and ate the night before.

The farmer told me about it. He said that rat meat turned a cat's stomach sour. There is too much acid in the meat. Cats can take it; but they do, as a rule, get a little sick from it. The fresh milk provides a "coating" for their stomachs. That's the reason the farmer told me to give them all the milk they wanted. He wanted them to stay healthy.

So that's what I did. And that's why I did it. I enjoyed it for two reasons. One, it was good to see the cats enjoying themselves—catching their squirts of milk into their open mouths and then licking their whiskers. (They sometimes did acrobatics to catch the stream; but they always managed to be there.) I also enjoyed it because I felt like I was doing good. I was a kind of "junior veterinarian," helping to heal the queasy stomachs of a couple of good and useful cats.

Now what's the moral to this story? What does it tell you about growing up the right way? I'll give you a hint. Try to think of it in terms of your faith and the sacraments, especially Holy Communion. Take your time. I'll be right back.

MORAL OF THE STORY
As I see it, this story has to do with you living in your world. Think of your world—now and later on in life— as something like the world where the farm cats lived.

Of course, you'll never have to eat rat meat for food; but you will rub shoulders with individuals who are selfish, and you will meet groups of people who are full of hatred. Even though they disgust you now by the way they act, they do influence you. You "take in" their attitudes by just being around them.

That's why you need a "coating" for your soul, just as those farm cats needed a "coating" for their stomachs. Otherwise, you might get soured on life.

Your religion provides this "coating." The sacraments of Jesus are kind of an "insulation" for your insides. They give a healing. So does the knowledge of your faith that you get in religious education.

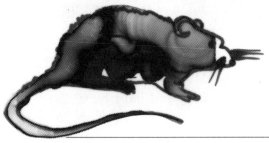

Unless you become a hermit, or somehow leave the world entirely, you are stuck with the good and the bad of what this world gives you. Much of it is good, of course. Don't lose hold of your ability to see what's good about the world or lose your drive to make the world better.

But many people in the world are bad. They are selfish, mean, bitter, ready to start a fight (or start a war) at any minute. This kind of behavior can get to you and tempt you to start thinking, "Everybody's doing it; I might as well do it too!"

Don't go down that route. Continue to learn more about your faith and grow in your love for the sacraments which nourish your faith. If you refuse to let yourself be fed by this "good milk" for your mind and soul, you'll end up being bitter about almost everything. Then you'll turn out to be just as mean as those people who are disgusting to you now.

That's no way to grow up. Be as smart as the farm cats in my story. Think of Holy Communion—and everything else you get from Jesus—as good "preventive medicine," keeping you healthy, inside and out.

And you will grow up good.

Tiger in Your Tank

The Story: While I'm on the subject of religion and faith, I want to tell you about another animal. This is not about a real tiger, though. It's a "make believe" one, thought up by advertisers. It sells gasoline and it seems to leap right into gas tanks and give engines extra power. The slogan is "Put a tiger in your tank."

The first time I remember hearing the slogan, I was working in advertising. That was just before I became a lumberjack and two years before I decided to be a priest. Being in the advertising business, I was especially sensitive to the way advertisers work.

You see, they have to make believe. Their job is to sell a product to the public. It would be difficult to be completely honest about what they are doing. It's not that they tell a lie, or anything like that. They just do all they can to put their product in the best light...to make you really want what they are selling.

So they don't say "Go out and buy our gasoline!" That would be too *blah*, too ordinary. They turn the gasoline into a tiger—a sure-footed, powerful tiger. Customers think they are getting all the strength and power and sureness that a tiger can give. It's a trick of "let's pretend."

Other advertisers pretend with humans instead of animals. One fruit company dressed up a banana. They wanted to sell lots of them. Bananas are all the same—bunch after bunch—as they come from Central and

South America. But they don't say "Buy a bunch of bananas!" They take one banana and put her in front of the TV cameras, where she "communicates." She has a name: "I'm Chiquita Banana and I've come to say...."

"Mr. Clean" is not a "Mister" at all. It's a bottle of liquid cleanser that seems to be good for shining up a kitchen floor. But they don't say, "Buy one of our bottles of floor cleaners coming off our assembly line!" That's too straightforward. They put a bald head on the top of a bottle, and strong shoulders on the area where the bottle slopes. He looks like a helpful giant, making friends with babies, folding his arms and smiling with satisfaction over a kitchen job well done.

I'm sure you can come up with many more examples. Just recently, a girl in 4th grade told me, "I like the cereal called Snap, Crackle and Pop! She forgot the name Rice Krispies, but she knew the characters that "humanize" the product.

Then there's Ike, the lucky dog. I like this animal on TV. His name is the same as mine. And he looks something like me, too! Notice, in this commercial, the company is not selling dog food; it's selling Ike who is such a lucky dog because he enjoys that particular dog food.

On and on it goes. Advertisers are really smart. They can teach us something about growing up, especially about growing up in religion. They know all about the "personalized approach." I'll let you think about it for a while.

MORAL OF THE STORY

I admit, this lesson is a bit tricky. I wouldn't have mentioned that "tiger in the tank," or any of his other friends, if I didn't love Jesus so much. But I do. And so I did.

What comes to me, from all these advertising per-

sonalities, is a simple message. The characters in TV commercials make cold products warm and human. We should make our faith in Jesus Christ a warm and human thing, too.

Television commercials start off with a generalization—a tank-full of gasoline, a shipload of bananas, crates of liquid cleanser, a two-ton truck loaded with dog food. But they never leave things in bunches or boxes or stuff like that. They *zoom* into the particular. They make an animal, or a person, out of their product, and these "individuals" are the ones who communicate.

But what about us who believe in Jesus? Unlike advertisers, we don't have to fake it. We don't have to shove a tiger into a gas tank, or put a skirt on a banana, or pretend that a bottle of cleanser is a bald-headed man.

We start off with a person—a real, live, loving person—Jesus Christ. But so often we don't stay with the person, Jesus. Most of the time we think of our religion in terms of *Dos* and *Don'ts*—lists of what we "have to do" and "don't have to do"...and rules and regulations about "how much we can get away with before it's a sin."

Take one example. So many children (adults, too!) complain about going to Mass. "Do I *have to* go?" Often, the reply is, "Yes you *have to*."

That's true. To Catholics, it is an insult to a loving God to refuse to go to Mass. So it is wrong not to. But that's not the main reason why we go to Mass. We go because there is a person—Jesus Christ—who wants us to be there.

Jesus is more real than a tiger on TV, more warm and friendly than Mr. Clean, more lively than Snap, Crackle and Pop.

We must begin where our faith begins: with Jesus, who gives us his teaching in the Gospel and who gives us his own life in Holy Communion. We go to Mass so that he can do this for us and so that we can join him as he thanks God for everything that we have, and are, and hope to be.

It will add to your fun if you use your brains as you look at the ads on TV. Sure, enjoy their antics and their songs. But, at the same time, know that there is another person—Jesus Christ—who is not make believe. From now on, as you watch the commercials, think of Jesus at the same time. His friendliness is friendlier than any of them. His life is livelier. And his promises about happiness are better and much more true.

He is a person you can really put your faith in. Stay loyal to Jesus, and it's guaranteed that you will grow up good.

The Hunting Dog
in a Closed-Up Car

The Story: This is a story about a dog trained to be a hunter. I'm not sure what he hunted. I only met him once. I was hitchhiking home from California in 1947. (That was when hitchhiking was safe.)

A middle-aged man picked me up. He was alone, except for his dog in the back seat. It was a warm summer day. I began to roll the window down.

Two things happened at once. The dog immediately

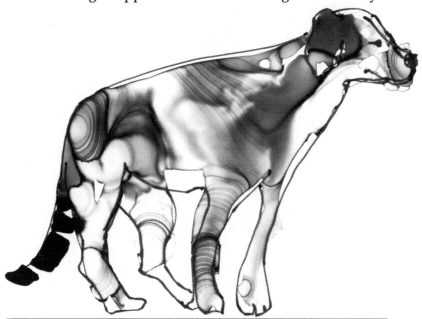

bounded for the open window—his eyes alert, shoulders trembling, nostrils shaking with excitement.

The other thing that happened was the driver's no-nonsense command to me to "Shut the window!" I did...and sweated out the rest of the trip.

I got out at the next town. Before I did, the driver explained about the closed windows:

"Dogs like to stick their heads out the window of a moving car. They take in all kinds of interesting things. A dog's nose is a sensitive instrument. It can tell him "animal stories" that are really fascinating. The instincts of a dog—especially a hunting dog—can sense all the other animals as the car goes by. The nose can run with the rabbits, jump with the deer, feel affection for other dogs, and shake with anger at all the cats and squirrels.

"It's very exciting. But it ruins a hunting dog. Hunters have to keep their dog's instincts for the times when it counts. If I let my Sheeba have all the excitement she wants, she'd become overstimulated. Her nose would get all clogged up from too many scents—too many rabbits and squirrels and deer. Then she'd be useless when I wanted her to help me hunt. I'm not going to spoil her with too many adventures. She'll have to learn discipline. And since she won't learn it on her own, I'm 'learning' it for her. That's why the windows are shut!"

And that's my story. What does it teach you about yourself? About growing up? I know you'll have some good ideas about this story. I won't wait too long. I'll just walk around the block once and then come back.

MORAL OF THE STORY

The idea I have is difficult to explain. Oh, I know what I'm talking about and I know it's important to me. But it's hard to put it in a few words. I'll do my best. Here goes:

As the hunter warned his dog to "Watch out for 'over-excitement' out the window—it will ruin your nose," I am warning you to "Watch out for 'over-excitement' on television—it will ruin your imagination."

Please understand. I'm not against TV. There's a lot of good learning and a lot of good stories in those tubes. I like TV myself. (I'm sure Jesus would like it too, and he would have used TV for telling his stories.)

What I'm talking about is the need for balance in your life and the absolute necessity for discipline. Sometimes this "discipline" means being able to be by yourself, and be silent. Sometimes, it means being able to be creative, even when you're bored and life isn't very interesting or lively.

If you *always* demand to be excited, you'll be as dumb as a dog who *always* has to have his face out the open

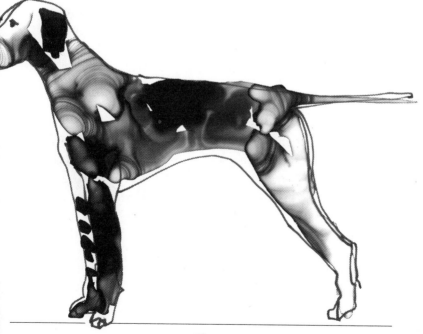

window of a car. If every minute of your day has to be given over to fun and games and TV and radio, you'll become overstimulated by life. This life won't be your *own* life, as though you had something to do with it. It is "life" that has been handed to you on a silver platter, without you doing any work at all. You just sit back and soak it in.

Then, when it comes time for you to use your own imagination, you won't know how. Your imagination will get flabby and your courage will go soft. As the hunting instincts of a dog become useless because of overexcitement, your creative instincts can do the same, unless, once in a while, you close the doors and shut the windows of your desire to be "turned on" all the time.

By the way, that's why so many teenagers take drugs or drink. They're all "burned out" inside themselves. Imagination is like a muscle. If you use it, and "train" it, it's healthy. If you don't use it, it's no good. Some teenagers haven't used their own imagination for a long time. When they were your age, they just took in what other people provided for them on the TV screen and in the streets.

Well, fun and games and television can get boring, too. Then they see nothing left for them but to go to the more risky stuff—cocaine, and other drugs. The fact is, they are bored with life and don't know how to do anything about it, on their own. So they keep trying to find new ways to get "unbored." And they end up in very bad shape.

Please don't be afraid of boredom. It's not *always* the worst thing that could happen to you. Sometimes, it can be the best thing. Ask grown-ups. They'll tell you that it was the times when they were most miserable—and when they felt lonely and left out of things—that they found out who they *really* were.

Try it the next time you are "down" with nothing to do. Relax. Settle yourself into your boredom. Chances are, you'll discover that you have more courage than you thought you had, and more creativity than you suspected.

You see, you have to develop balance in every part of your life. You do need friends. You also need stimulation provided by television, sports and the times when you get together to have fun.

But you also need some quiet time, independent of outside excitement. This quiet time is something like the closed-up car for that hunting dog. It's not very comfortable to be stuck with "nothing to do and nobody to do it with," but these occasions can allow you to get in touch with your own goodness and your own wisdom, independent of anybody else.

Don't be afraid of the times when your life isn't exciting. Unless you can "handle" loneliness, you'll never be able to make real friends. And unless you can live with boredom—*sometimes* —you won't be as creative as you could be.

Put balance in your life when you are young. This will make it easier for you to be good when you grow up.

"You Can Lead a Horse to Water, But..."

The Story: This story is about a slogan I don't like very much. It's also about a big red-haired horse I liked a lot. And it's about a year in my life that I really loved.

The year is June 1952 to April 1953. I was 23 years old. I thought maybe I was supposed to be a Passionist and a priest. But I wasn't sure. When I was in New York City, the priest I went to see about this question told me, "Son, before you come to any decision, you'll have to find out whether or not you can handle loneliness."

This seemed like good advice. I left my job in advertising. Then I travelled north and west, filling up my time with odd jobs, new friends, different places, some loneliness and a lot of silence. I ended up as a lumberjack in Canada—Northern Ontario. The lumber camp was a rugged wilderness of white pines. We cut down trees in the old style—no power machines, no bulldozers—just pulleys and the two-man saw and the double-blade axe, and horses to drag the logs. There were almost a hundred horses in the camp.

One of these horses—I named him Barnaby—was my favorite. I always made a point of "watering" him. Others had to be cared for, too. But Barnaby was served first.

He was bigger than the others. His red coat seemed to

catch all of the winter sun. His sides and shoulders were always warm, even when it was 30 below zero.

Before we walked back to camp, I'd lead him down to the river's edge, break the ice on the surface, lower down the reins, and lean against his side to warm my face while he bent down for great gulps of the clear cold water. It's wonderful to hear a big horse drink and feel his pleasure in it!

Sure he drank. All of them drank. They were thirsty They had been working hard all day!

That's why I don't like the slogan: "You can lead a horse to water, but you can't make him drink." It goes against my ex- perience. I could always lead Barnaby to water and make him drink. I did so by mak- ing him work, first—skidding logs and pulling stumps and do- ing other things that got his harness all sweaty. Then I broke the ice and let his neck drop down, and I knew what he would do. I knew that he would drink!

So the slogan doesn't work for horses. It doesn't work for hu- mans, either, in one sense. I could "make" anybody drink. I'd need a little help, maybe, but I could do it. How? I would put the person into a sweat-box for a while, or put him in an exercise belt. After an hour of this, that person would drink. He or she's thirsty. (The body is sending a message, "I need it.")

However, there is one situation when the slogan does hold true for people. But that has to do with the moral of the story, not the story itself. I'll wait 'til then.

MORAL OF THE STORY

As I see it, the moral is this:"Whenever you are thirsty—'thirsty' in whatever way—be as smart as the horse Barnaby and find a way to quench your thirst."

This advice may seem unnecessary when you first read it. It's just common sense. Babies know enough to yell when they are thirsty, and they keep yelling until the bottle comes.

But there are other kinds of "thirsts" which are more difficult to understand than physical thirst. All people have a deep need to feel that they are accepted, they are loved, they are *somebody important*. These are "thirsts."

Also, we all have a need to be able to relax. We cannot be constantly pressured by too many demands on us. So we thirst for peace as well as for appreciation. And unless we can find a good way to satisfy these thirsts, our whole system gets upset.

Sometimes, people refuse to admit that their "thirst systems" are upset. They don't face up honestly to their needs. They escape into alcoholism, or drug addiction, or overeating, or something else. Sometimes they "take it out on others" by making life miserable at home. Such escapes don't satisfy them. They only cause them to get hung up by bad habits.

These are the situations when that slogan is true. Nothing in life is more saddening, or more frustrating, than to see anybody get so stubborn that he or she refuses to get help.

It seems that Barnaby was a lot wiser than some humans are. A lot more healthy, too. I hope you understand this. I hope you always have the kind of "horse sense" that Barnaby had.

Sometimes, when you work hard, or worry a lot, or (in whatever way) put yourself under pressure, these things can build up stress. And you feel maybe that you are *not* loved, *not* appreciated, *not* at peace. You've felt this strain already, at times. As you get older, you'll feel it again and again. This can drain you. It's something like "working up a sweat" when you play ball. Only this kind of sweat—the "sweat" produced by stress—is harder to see. It's on the inside. It's emotional and psychological, and sometimes spiritual.

Whenever this happens to you, be honest enough to admit it. Instead of finding "escapes" from it, find some good friends who will help you understand that you do have many good things going for you and that life isn't all bad and that there are people in the world who really can appreciate you. There's nothing wrong in admitting you need the help of friends.

And don't forget to pray. God is a good friend, too. God will help you put peace and hope back in your heart again.

All this is a part of the work of growing up—knowing what your "thirsts" are and knowing where to go to quench these thirsts. It's a matter of horsesense, of a horse named Barnaby.

The Calves Need Boundaries

The Story: We're back on the farm again. This is my second favorite memory about the time I worked on that small dairy farm near Oswego, N.Y.

I wasn't much older than you are now. There were some calves born that spring, about 5 or 6 of them. By the time I started to work, they were big enough to walk around on their own, and to eat food without too much benefit from their mother's milk. And they were strong—almost as strong as I was. I learned that fast enough. (But I'm ahead of my story. I better back up.)

From the time these calves were born until the time I met them, they were stuck inside the barn—first, to be nursed by their Momma-cow, then tucked away in their own corner, eating their own dull cereal of stale hay. Not very appetizing! But they didn't know anything different at the time, so that's what they did.

Then came the day for their wonderful new adventure. They were ready to go outdoors and enjoy all the good fresh grass and clover. I was told to lead them out to their paradise, and I had the pleasure of watching them enjoy themselves with their new diet.

First, however, I had to teach them a lesson. They had to learn about boundaries. The pastureland was wide and it was long. But there was the danger of rocks (which could break their legs) on the side of the woods. And there was the danger of getting hit by a car on the side by the state road. Because of these dangers, the farmer put up an electric-wire fence all around. The fence sent out a message: "The whole territory inside this fence is okay; but the world outside this fence is a"no no!" This "no no" had a shock to it so that the animals would never forget the message.

Well, I had to drag the calves—one by one—over to the fence. Before they were free to enjoy their new paradise, I had to show them what it felt like if they disobeyed the "no no." It wasn't fun. I caused them to suffer. I pulled them by the neck, and pulled them, and pulled them. Finally we got close and then I'd stick the tip of their nose right into the wire, so they could feel the force of that hurting electric shock on the most sensitive part of their bodies.

It was hard work, let me tell you. The calves were confused. They had never been treated this way, dragged around by force. They fought me with every ounce of strength they had. And they squealed and squeaked, their bodies shivered, and their eyes got big and teary. It was as though they sensed that they were being dragged to their doom. And they didn't like it, not one bit!

Then wham! Their nose got a powerful shock and they let out a terrible cry!

Right after that, I let them go. Then came the fun part of the job. I smiled as I saw them get used to their new surroundings. They walked around in a daze for a few seconds. Then they noticed the fresh grass, and started chomping away. Obviously, they were very pleased with their new food. (You would be, too, if you were forced to eat stale cereal for six months; and then you were introduced to pizza or ice cream or whatever it is that you like best.)

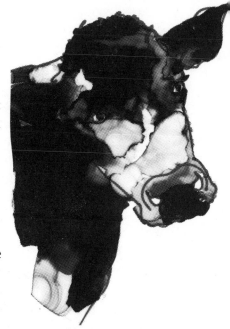

After they grazed on the grass for a while, they then noticed all the room they had. And they ran and kicked their legs all-which-ways, and ate some more, and chased their friends, and ran around in big circles...just like little children at recess, having the time of their lives.

But they never forgot the lesson about boundaries. They soon forgot the pain on the tip of their nose, but they always remembered where the pain came from. The point is, though, that the pain itself had gone. They couldn't think of a little thing like that when they were having so much fun.

That's my story. You tell me the moral of the story. What does it mean for you, in terms of you growing up? I know you'll get one lesson from it. I have two of them. Think about it for a while. I'm going to the kitchen to get a glass of milk.

MORAL OF THE STORY
I know you figured out the first moral. Young people always do. Yes, there has to be boundaries for you, too.

And sometimes it hurts to learn about them.

Sometimes you get punished, or "grounded," because you overstepped the rules. There's a certain gang of kids you shouldn't hang around with...and you did. There's a certain time you should have been home...and you weren't. You have schoolwork to do and jobs at home to finish—like it or not. You must balance the time for fun with time for things that aren't so much fun. Things like that.

You know this. Life would be impossible without limits. Grownups know this, too. When they get married, for instance, or take on a new job, they get limited. They can't be everything, or do everything, or marry everybody! Older people also (like your grandparents) get limited by their age. That's a kind of boundary. They don't have the health, or the strength, to do what they used to do. That's life.

Don't waste your time getting bitter about your limits. Those calves at springtime couldn't understand the reason why I was hurting them on the tip of their noses. I did so because I loved them. I didn't want them to get *really* hurt by getting run over, or breaking their legs on the rocks.

You are better than those dumb animals. You *can* understand why you get punished, sometimes, and why you get dragged into doing what you don't want to do. You're learning about boundaries the hard way. We all have to learn about boundaries, one way or another.

But at least the calves had sense enough to be so happy about their fresh-grown grass, and having fun in their pastureland, that they didn't even give a thought to the shock they got from the electric fence.

You ought to have at least as much sense as that. Don't dwell on your hurts or punishments, or on being told what your limits are. Look around you and notice all the good things you *really* do have, in the "pasture-land" where you live and walk and play and go to school.

There is one more moral to this story. It has to do with people who don't like you. Say it's a neighbor who is a grouch. Say it's somebody your own age, or a little older, who teases you or bullies you, or for some reason doesn't like you. Don't let these characters ruin your life. Consider the bad things they do to you to be like a painful shock hurting your nose. The hurt of it won't last. There will always be certain people who won't like you, no matter what you do.

I'm not saying don't let it hurt you. It does hurt. Just don't let them get you down. Do what the calves did after they got hurt. Look around at all the friends you *do* have, and all the enjoyment the *rest* of your life can give you.

That way you can forget the "stings" you receive from bullies and bad luck. Look at the *whole picture* of your life, and you won't get so upset about the way life shocks you, sometimes.

And you will grow up good.

Beware of Chickadee Friends

The Story: This is a short-short animal story. But it has a big moral—that is, big in importance. It will be important to you as long as your life will last.

Follow me back in time to the lumbercamp in Northern Canada when I was 23 years old. There was only one animal left to look at during that hard winter. Big animals, like bears, were hibernating in caves. Fish stayed under the ice. Wolves you could hear, but you could never see them. All the birds were long-gone to warmer climates. All but one. This was the "mascot" of the lumberjacks—the little chickadees.

They are pretty birds, the chickadees. And friendly, too. (They seemed to be.) They would follow us like pet dogs on a country walk as we started out, in the early morning to chop down trees.

They would fly from bush to tree to bush, right beside us, during the whole trip. Sometimes you could almost touch them, they were that close. And they had a cheerful song to sing, to put us in a good mood. You've heard their song. Over and over, like a happy tune: "CHICK a DEE...DEEdee...CHICK a DEE DEEdee...."

Like cheerleaders along the sideline of a football game, these birds would be spurring us on, giving us a life to our mornings, making us feel good because they seemed to be so happy with their chick-a-dee dee-dee!

I thought they were my friends. I thought they trav-

eled along with me because they liked me.

But I was wrong. After a while, I learned that they followed me only because of what they could get out of me. You see, the favorite meal of the chickadees is the worms and grubs that live between the bark and the trunk of a pine tree. These little birds are not equipped with the beak of a woodpecker, so they cannot dig out this food for themselves. That's why they rely on lumberjacks to do their work for them. As soon as we cut down a tree, they'd have a feast!

It really hurt me when I found this out. I felt "used" by an animal I thought was my friend. I felt a let down, as though the wind went out of my sails.

I think the reason why I felt so bad was because the chickadees reminded me of certain people who treated me in much the same way. I remembered those who had been my friends. (*I thought* they were my friends.) But then I discovered that they had been just using me for their own selfish purposes. So I felt bad about the chickadees because I still felt so bad about some "human chickadees" who had let me down.

That's my story. In a way, I already mentioned the

moral of the story. I'm sure you have already started to think about people in your life who have "used" you and hurt your feelings. And you felt bad about it. And maybe you still feel bad because certain "friends" turned out to be *not*-your-friends.

Yes, but that's only part of what I want to say about this story. There's another part—very important for your growing up. I haven't mentioned it yet. See if you can guess what it might be.

MORAL OF THE STORY
One moral is something you already know. You've been hurt by people you thought were your friends. And then

you found out differently. They used you, or betrayed you, or somehow let you down. This hurts. It hurts when grownups disappoint you, especially when they say they love you, but then you find out they are thinking only of themselves. Sometimes it hurts even worse when you get pushed away by boys and girls your own age.

That's life! There already have been individuals who turned out to be "chickadees." There always will be people like that, as long as you live. Nothing much you can do about it. You can't force anybody to be different from what they decided to be. The moral of the story is that you just have to live with the facts of life—there will be people who will cause you sadness.

But the other moral to the story is this: don't let false friends sour you on the rest of the world. Not everybody will cause you sadness.

I remember, during a Parish Mission, telling this story. Then I asked the children to tell me the moral of the story. A boy in fifth grade answered. His words were very soft...and, though he wasn't crying, his eyes were a little wet. He said this: "Never trust a friend!"

He only said those four words. But he said plenty. He was very hurt because a friend of his had turned against him in some way.

My heart went out to him. But I had to say something. I didn't want to let his decision "not to trust anybody" stay with him all his life.

I replied, "Yes, it hurts. It's not supposed to not-hurt." But that does not mean you can't trust the other friends you have.

"We can't get down on life and be suspicious of everybody just because some people give us a bad time. We've got to keep our courage up, and keep remembering that some people still deserve our love.

"If we don't, we'll shrivel up into our own little world and we'll sulk and mope and distrust everybody. Then we'll lose out on the friends who want to be our true friends. And we'll end up miserable and very lonely.

"We can't do that. Be hurt when those you thought were your friends have turned out to be selfish chickadees. Yes. I don't blame you for being hurt. I get hurt when it happens to me. But you can't let these feelings drive hope out of your heart. You have to keep trusting in life...and in God (who will never let you down)...and in the friends you still do have."

That's what I said then. That's what I say now. To continue to live with hope and trust—even when you are hurting—*that's* what it means to grow up.

Mockingbirds Are Bad News

The Story: This animal story is not just something that happened to me. I guess it has happened to everybody. But maybe not. I better speak only for myself.

Some people like mockingbirds. Admittedly, these creatures do have a wide variety in the songs they sing. They can imitate just about all the tunes that any bird has ever come up with. They love to perch on a tree branch or telephone pole, puff up their chests, and pretend they are a robin, or meadowlark, or cardinal, or grackle, or something else.

As I say, some people enjoy the variety. I, for one, can't stand them! They are too loud. They try too hard to be taken for somebody else. And (as far as I can tell) they are bullies.

Almost every other bird I like. I'm somewhat disappointed with chickadees, as I already told you. But I still enjoy their song. I don't like bluejays, because they're bullies, too. But all the other birds—from sparrows to ospreys to eagles—I love them all.

Mockingbirds, however, are bad news. They make too much noise, for one thing. I've lived in places where they start yakking and yakking (I won't call it singing!) at three o'clock in the morning! They wake me up and then I can't go back to sleep.

If they only would sing in the same way as the birds they copy. But their version is a *mockery* of other birds, not a gracious imitation. It's almost like hearing an ugly "shout-out" of a pretty song.

Sometimes I think they are trying too hard to belong to another flock of birds. They don't want to be themselves. (I've never heard the bird sing anything original.) They want to be somebody else. I don't like that in any creature—bird or human!

Then sometimes I think they turn up their volume because they are bullies. They make fun of other birds in order to drive them crazy so that they can take over the whole territory and feast themselves on the eggs that are left in the nest.

That's happened in our lovely monastery in West Springfield, Massachusetts. When it's early spring, we have bluebirds, redbirds, wild canaries, cardinals, scarlet tanagers, and lots more. Then come the mockingbirds and the blue jays. Their bullying tactics drive away almost all the others and we're stuck with their bothersome noise all summer long.

There are a couple of morals to this story. It's easy to think up one of them—don't you become a "mockingbird." The other moral is a little more tricky. It has to do with anger (anger is okay, sometimes), and with being choosey about how to pick your friends.

Think about it for a while. I'm going to fill the bird feeder, hoping some cardinals will come back.

MORAL OF THE STORY

Sure, you already hit upon the first lesson: "Don't try too hard to belong to a group of friends if that group makes you pretend to be somebody else, other than who you are. "

It'll never work. You'll end up being as phoney as a mockingbird mimicking a song sparrow. Don't surrender the best that's in you just to be accepted. Never try to be what you aren't. You'll end up being false to yourself.

Don't be like a girl putting on heavy makeup so she can look older, or like a boy strutting around and talking big so he can look older. That's the behavior of a mockingbird who is too loud, too pushy, not real, and doesn't fool anybody.

You already know this. Another lesson to the story is that it's okay, sometimes, to be angry. And it's certainly okay to pick and choose your friends.

As far as anger is concerned, look at Jesus. He was angry, sometimes. He made whips and really used them when people went to the Temple in Jerusalem and were not respectful to God his Father. And he got angry at the Pharisees when they were phoneys. "Hypocrites" he called them. (By the way, they got very angry at him because he showed them up. Matter of fact, when Jesus was crucified, the Pharisees were jeering at him just like a bunch of hateful mockingbirds! The same thing can happen to you. When you show up phonies for being phonies, they will get mad at you. Don't worry about it. They did the same thing to Jesus.)

Also, Jesus chose his friends with care. He loved everybody. But he spent more time with his Apostles than he did with those enemies of his who were out to get him.

So it's okay to be angry at people who are phonies. It's okay to get mad at those who hurt other people. Just keep control of your anger. Don't turn into a bully yourself. Don't end up as bad as they are.

And finally, in choosing your friends, don't feel bad because there are some people you can't be friends with. You can't like them all, any more than I can like all the birds in the sky.

In many cases, it's not your fault. It's their fault, because they are mean or cruel or something. It may be that you don't want to get close to them because they seem to bring out the worst in you. Okay. Use your head. Don't associate with them, if you can help it. Be grateful for the good friends you have—those who bring out the best in you, and who let you bring out the best in them.

There will always be "mockingbird people" in your life. There will always be good people, too. The trick is to learn which is which. It's all a part of growing up.

Monkeys Hang on Too Long

The Story: This is a story about monkeys in Africa. I tell it to everyone, people of all ages. (Perhaps you can tell it to your parents and other grownups. See if they can figure out the moral.)

A nun who was a missionary in Africa told me this story about 20 years ago. I forget just where in Africa it was. The place is not important. She told me how the natives caught monkeys. They captured them, then shipped them off to zoos all over the world. That's the only way they earned money. That's the only way they survived.

They had a simple way of doing it. They would take a gourd (which is shaped something like a pumpkin) and hollow out the inside from the hole made on top. Then they would patch up this hole and cut a smaller hole at the side of the gourd—a hole just big enough to let a monkey's hand squeeze through. If you think of a birdhouse with an opening a little larger than a normal birdhouse, you have the picture of it.

Next, the natives dropped some peanuts inside the gourd. Then they tied these to trees all around the village. Then they went back home. Everything quieted down. The coast was clear.

All the while, the monkeys were up in the trees, watching the whole thing. They love peanuts. As soon as they had the place to themselves, they would climb

down, push their hand through the opening, and reach in to get a fistful of peanuts.

But when they tried to get their treasure out, they couldn't move. The fist was too big to go through the hole. The only way they could leave was the same way they entered—squeeze the hand out as they had squeezed the hand in. But first they had to drop the peanuts.

They would not do it! They wanted those peanuts so badly they wouldn't let go. They stayed there—all night long—screaming their lungs out with rage and fear. Then the natives picked them up the next morning. The monkeys were dropped in cages, then shipped off to zoos all over the world. They lived behind bars the rest of their lives—very unhappy and very un-free.

Dumb, huh? You feel like shouting at them, "You stupid monkeys! Let go of the peanuts. Just let go! And you will be free—free to swing in trees, and eat bananas, and pick fleas from your buddy's hair—and have all kinds of fun. But you have to drop those peanuts!"

That is precisely what they refused to do. It's sad, the way they ended up. These monkeys made a very bad mistake and they lived to regret it.

That's my story. I've done my work. Now it's your turn. You think up the moral to the story. It won't take you long. There are all kinds of lessons to learn from it. You've got your ideas. I've got mine. We'll both be right. Think about yours, first. Then I'll come back and tell you my idea.

MORAL OF THE STORY
I'm sure the lesson you came up with was good. I'm also pretty sure it wasn't the same as mine. The reason is because you're young and I'm older. You still have a lot of "bounce" to you; and you don't let your hurt feelings get you down for long. You don't stay sulking for days and days. When somebody insults you, or refuses to talk to you, or gives you a put-down, you probably go away for a while. You sulk a little and feel sorry for yourself. But you don't stay down. After a short time, you "bounce back" and the hurts are soon forgotten. I sure hope that's true.

Some teenagers, though, don't have the same bounce-back-ability. Some grownups don't, either. That's why there are so many suicides in the world.

And there are a lot more things I call "mini-suicides"—"little deaths." Some people don't go so far as to kill themselves. They don't say *"no!"* to their life that permanently. But they do quit on life in smaller ways— by getting hooked on drugs, or drink, or by not speaking to people much, or by getting soft and flabby because of overeating or watching TV all the time. Things like that.

Usually, the reason they ruin their life is because somebody hurt their feelings and they "can't get over it." All they do is remember how unfairly they were treated. And they get bitter and bad-tempered and they don't want to cheer up.

People who react like this are just as stupid as those monkeys in Africa. They held on to their peanuts and wouldn't let go. Some people hold on to their hurts and won't let go of them. Because they won't stop thinking

about it, they put themselves into the prisons of their own hurt feelings. And that means they are not free any more.

Don't grow up to be this kind of a person. Learn early to let go of all the reasons (even when you think they are *good* reasons) to feel miserable.

The most basic lesson Jesus taught us is that we *must* forgive those who have treated us badly. He didn't say we had to forget the hurt. (Sometimes we can't forget, at least, not for a while.) He said we had to forgive.

And Jesus didn't say we had to pretend it doesn't hurt. He was hurt, too, when he was judged unfairly and when they beat him up and crucified him. He was deeply hurt when people did not accept him. He even wept because he felt so badly. But this sadness never stopped him from loving those who remained faithful to him. He still loved and trusted God, even when everything around him was full of hatred.

Unfair treatment never stopped Jesus. And it can't stop you. Don't let it. Certain people—old and young—have already hurt you. That's life.

But you don't call it quits because there is wickedness around you. You must forgive those who have wronged you in any way. Do so for the sake of your own freedom—the freedom to live in the real world of your present time, with all the goodness that is available to you.

You must "let go of your peanuts" and get on with the job of living. That's what it takes to *really* grow up.

Why Does a Gorilla
Beat His Chest?

A Riddle: This is the last chapter. It's different. It's still about animals. But, instead of a story with a moral, it's a riddle, and the lesson to be learned is in the answer to the riddle.

The riddle is this:

Whenever there is a "showdown" among the big beasts of the jungle,

Why does the gorilla beat his chest?

Why does the elephant blow his trumpet?

Why do the big cats snarl?

"Why?"

The answer is easy, once you put a little thought to it. Each animal is pointing out the one thing that makes them different. Among the big animals, only gorillas can stand up straight. That's why they beat their chests—to show how free their arms are, and the other animals better watch out!

The elephant's special gift is the long, strong trunk. And so, when there's danger, elephants blow away like a trumpet player. They are pointing out their sign—the special gift of power which is theirs alone.

Lions and tigers and other cats have their speciality. Their power is in their teeth. And so they snarl when a

showdown comes. They're pointing out what makes them so powerful, so special.

That's my riddle. Now what's the point? I am talking to you as Christians—believers in Jesus Christ. What is your sign of Christianity? What marks you off as being special, having the "power to face up to a showdown" that other people don't have?

The answer to this is the most important lesson of all, in terms of your growing up.

ANSWER TO THE RIDDLE

There is one sign of Christianity—one and only one. The sign that we are followers of Christ is not a picture of Jesus hugging a little child, or Jesus picking up garbage that has made a mess of some picnic grounds, or Jesus building a hospital or leading a cause for social justice.

Of course, we know that Jesus loved children. He still does. And all you have to do is listen to his parables to know that he loved nature and animals. And he does not want nature to get spoiled by human thoughtlessness; he does not want animals to be treated cruelly.

And Jesus cared—very much—about healing people who are sick and depressed. He cured thousands himself. Also he is very angry about injustice, wherever it happens. Indeed, he told us all that we will be happy in heaven or cursed to hell depending upon how we work to relieve those who suffer from hunger, or poverty, or wars, or any of the ways that powerful people use poor people in order to get richer and more powerful.

But there are many unbelievers who love children. Christians don't have a monopoly on that. And many pagans, as well as Christians, care about the natural resources of the earth. And there are good men and women all over the world—even some who are opposed to Christianity—who spend their whole lives helping those who suffer from sickness and poverty and oppression.

However, there is one gift—one special gift—that only a Christian has. There is one problem that nobody else has the answer to. That's why it is our sign—the *Sign of the Cross.*

What is it that we do when Catholics make the sign of the cross? We are remembering what happened to Jesus, when he died on the cross in order to prove his love for us and in order to give us his life. The life he gives us is the life he is living now, in heaven.

Nobody else has ever given us a satisfactory answer to why we suffer...and especially to why we have to die.

Many non-Christians are very good people. Many are better, really, than we are. And God loves them. But, without the Sign of the Cross, they are not much good about handling the mystery of death. Jesus is the only one who has given us the answer to the toughest problem of them all.

I wouldn't go into this serious problem if I thought you were just a child. You have thought deep thoughts about life already. (The very fact that you've read this book proves my statement. If you were "just a kid" you would have stopped reading, pages back.) But you have thought seriously about life; and you do want to know more about growing up.

The answer to suffering and death is part of growing up. Death is the biggest part of all. Many people go through life pretending they won't die. They just want to keep going, on and on, taking in all the fun and excitement they can, and not thinking about the future. They don't even want to hear of the possibility that they will get old, and slow down and, someday, they will die. But they *will* die. It is foolish of them to pretend they won't.

One way or another, you have already been forced to wrestle with the mystery of death. Maybe a friend was killed by a car or by disease. Maybe you remember the death of one of your parents or grandparents. You loved them. Now you miss them. And maybe you wonder why they had to die. And maybe you got angry at God for taking them.

These are all normal, natural reactions. But getting angry at God and missing somebody you love cannot be the only things you feel. You are a follower of Christ. And your sign is the *Sign of the Cross*. And so you know, by faith, that death is not the final thing that happens to anybody. Neither is suffering.

Jesus suffered ahead of us. He died on the Cross for our sakes. Then he rose from death to free us from the hold that sin has on us. And also—and more to the point I'm making here—he rose from death in order to raise us up.

Life, not death, is at the end of things. After you die, you will go to a place where you will live life fuller, and more joyfully, than you can even begin to imagine here on earth.

Remember this, please. If you don't remember anything else I've said, remember this. As I already explained, it's only when the jungle animals are challenged— when the "chips are down" —that they show their special gifts.

With humans, the biggest challenge of life is the fact of death. When you watch somebody you love die—and then when you die—that's the time you need an answer to: "What's the meaning of life?" "Is this all there is?" "Do we live for a while and then die...and that's all?"

It is at such a time you must stand up, with faith in Jesus Christ. And, like the gorilla beating his chest to show how free his arms are, you make your sign—the Sign of the Cross—and you know there is an everlasting life of Perfect Happiness waiting for you beyond the grave...already given you and prepared for you by Jesus.

So you don't have to let the fact of death crush you with its sadness or cause you to quit on life. You continue with hope and optimism...because you have been signed with the Sign of the Cross.